Transporte público
Public Transportation

¡VAMOS A TOMAR

EL TRANSBORDADOR!

LET'S TAKE THE

FERRY!

Elisa Peters

Traducido por Eida de la Vega

PowerKiDS press

New York

For Julie, in celebration of many trips on the Steamship Authority

Published in 2015 by The Rosen Publishing Group, Inc.
29 East 21st Street, New York, NY 10010

First Edition

Spanish translation: Eida de la Vega

Editor: Amelie von Zumbusch
Photo Research: Katie Stryker
Book Design: Andrew Povolny

Photo Credits: Cover James A. Harris/Shutterstock.com; p. 5 Mablache/iStock/Thinkstock; p. 6 Egdigital/iStock/Thinkstock; p. 9 Onepony/iStock/Thinkstock; p. 10 guroldinneden/Shutterstock.com; p. 13 iofoto/Shutterstock.com; p. 14 Philip Lange/Shutterstock.com; p. 17 Boomer Jerritt/All Canada Photos/Getty Images; p. 18 Marcus Clarkson/iStock/Thinkstock; p. 21 George White Location Photography/Photolibrary/Getty Images; p. 22 Dirk Heuer/Flickr/Getty Images.

Publisher's Cataloging Data

Peters, Elisa.
Let's take the ferry! = ¡Vamos a tomar el transbordador! / by Elisa Peters, translated by Eida de la Vega — first edition.
p. cm. — (Public transportation = Transporte público)
Parallel title: Transporte público
In English and Spanish.
Includes index.
ISBN 978-1-4777-6783-2 (library binding)
1. Ferries — Juvenile literature. I. Peters, Elisa. II. Title.
HE5751.P48 2015
386-d23

Websites: Due to the changing nature of Internet links, PowerKids Press has developed an online list of websites related to the subject of this book. This site is updated regularly. Please use this link to access the list: www.powerkidslinks.com/putr/ferry/

Manufactured in the United States of America

CPSIA Compliance Information: Batch #WS14PK4: For Further Information contact Rosen Publishing, New York, New York at 1-800-237-9932

Contenido

Contents

Un **transbordador** es un barco. Viaja por una ruta fija.

A **ferry** is a boat. It travels along a set route.

Algunos transbordadores transportan solo personas. Otros, cargan autos y camiones.

Some ferries carry just people. Others carry cars and trucks, too.

La parte delantera de un transbordador es la **proa**.
La parte trasera es la popa.

The front of a ferry is the **bow**.
The back is the stern.

En un transbordador, "babor" es el lado izquierdo. "Estribor", es el lado derecho.

"Port" means "left" on a ferry. "Starboard" means "right."

Algunos transbordadores son grandes y otros son más pequeños.

Some ferries are big. Others are smaller.

¡Los transbordadores pueden ir rápido! Su velocidad se mide en nudos.

Ferries can be fast! Their speed is measured in knots.

La tripulación trabaja en el transbordador.
El **capitán** es el jefe de la tripulación.

The crew works on the ferry.
The **captain** is the head of the crew.

El transbordador de Staten Island está en la ciudad de Nueva York. Es el de más uso en los Estados Unidos.

The Staten Island Ferry is in New York City. It is the busiest US ferry.

Una flota es un conjunto de barcos. El estado de Washington tiene la mayor flotilla de transbordadores de los Estados Unidos.

A fleet is a group of boats. Washington State has the biggest ferry fleet in the United States.

Viajar en transbordador es divertido. ¡Hay vistas maravillosas desde el agua!

It is fun to take a ferry. You get great views from the water!

PALABRAS QUE DEBES SABER / WORDS TO KNOW

(la) proa

bow

**(el) capitán/
(la) capitana**

captain

(el) transbordador

ferry